SELLING ACROSS BORDERS

PRUDHVI POLAVARAPU

INDIA · SINGAPORE · MALAYSIA

ISBN

Paperback 979-8-89475-990-6

Hardcase 979-8-89519-885-8

CONTENTS

Chapter 1

INTRODUCTION TO CROSS-BORDER SELLING

1.1. WHY CROSS-BORDER SELLING MATTERS

Selling products across borders in the Gulf Cooperation Council (GCC) region isn't just a fancy idea — it's a smart way to unlock amazing chances for your business.

Most people don't really know about this, and even those who do might feel a bit scared to try it out. But there are people out there who have cracked the code.

They understand the game and are taking advantage of it, making lots of money by selling to high-value individuals. Even if you're already selling big on platforms like Flipkart where prices really matter, why settle for that when you could sell the same thing in the GCC and make 3X the profit?

Business people are pretty clever.

If there is a scope of making good money, they won't just let it slip away.

But, of course, there's a catch: there are challenges that can make selling in the GCC look difficult. I'd be lying if I said these challenges weren't real. But don't worry, they're not unbeatable problems.

In this book, I'm going to walk you through the things that might otherwise give you trouble when you try to start e-commerce in GCC . You're going to learn how to handle these challenges and make your dream of doing E-commerce in GCC true .

The GCC countries are like a treasure chest full of chances for your business, but not everyone sees it that way. Some folks don't even know about it, and some are a bit scared of it. But then there are the smart ones who see it and understand that it's like a goldmine waiting to be explored.

You might already be selling like a pro on places like Amazon , Flipkart, and other indian Market places. where they care a lot about how much things cost. That's cool and all, but why stop there? The GCC is a place where people want high-quality products, and they're willing to pay for it. So, if you're selling something people want there, you can make way more profits than you ever thought possible.

Every business has its problems, and selling products in different countries is no exception. It's okay to be worried about it, but don't let it scare you too much. The problems might seem huge, but they're not impossible to solve. With a bit of knowledge and the right tricks up your sleeves, you can beat these challenges and come out on top.

Selling products across borders can feel like walking through a maze – confusing and tricky.

You might wonder:

How do I send things to other countries?

What about the rules and laws?

How do I educate the people there about my products?

These are good questions, and I'm here to help you find the answers.

As we go on this journey together, you'll see that every challenge is like a puzzle piece that fits into making your business better.

You'll learn about what people in the GCC like, how to make shipping work, how to tell the world about your products, and more. This book is like a toolkit to help you do well in the GCC market.

1.2. BENEFITS AND CHALLENGES OF CROSS-BORDER SELLING

If you are someone who's already doing well in the Indian market then you're sitting in the perfect spot to dive into cross-border selling. You've already tackled the hard part, and now the exciting journey awaits. But if you are new, then also you have an advantage that I will talk about soon.

For those of you who've already set up an e-commerce shop, congratulations!

You've climbed that initial mountain of challenges.

The good news is that this experience gives you a massive advantage in stepping into the world of cross-border selling. You've done the groundwork, and that's a big deal. No need to spend more money to start all over again. You can expand your existing business into new territories without reinventing the wheel.

If you're currently making twice the money you put in through your domestic sales, you're on the right track. Now, as you venture into the GCC market, that profit could soar even higher – maybe even ten times higher!

However, a lot of people have taken the plunge into cross-border selling and ended up disappointed. The culprit? Shipping. It might sound strange, but if you don't have a shipping partner who's a good match for your business, things can go south pretty quickly.

There are some other things to think about too, especially when it comes to your product.

The first important thing is that your product should be a unique niche. It's just one of those things that can make a real difference in how well your product is received.

Another critical point is understanding the GCC market. You need to know what's selling and what's not in that part of the world.

Don't worry – I'll give you a hand in figuring out market trends so that you're not shooting in the dark.

Now, if you're someone who's just starting to think about starting a business and you're not sure what to sell yet, listen up. This is a golden opportunity for you too. Knowing what sells like hotcakes in the GCC market can save you a lot of time and money. You won't end up investing a huge chunk of your hard-earned money in something that's not likely to make waves.

1.3. MARKET TRENDS AND OPPORTUNITIES

The transition from traditional brick-and-mortar stores to the realm of e-commerce was a gradual journey for the Middle East. However, what has truly caught my attention is the remarkable evolution that has turned this region into a dynamic hub for e-commerce enterprises.

Understanding this evolution takes us back to the year 2016, a time when merely 15% of businesses in the Middle East had ventured into the online space. It's astounding to realise that almost 90% of online purchases during that period involved products shipped from abroad. This intriguing statistic sheds light on distinct consumer behaviour, emphasising the allure of goods originating from different corners of the world.

Fast forward to the year 2022, and you witness a transformation that borders on the extraordinary. E-commerce sales in the Middle East have surged to an impressive $48.6 billion. This staggering number marks a nearly twofold increase from the $26.9 billion recorded in the year 2018. This growth trajectory is not just indicative of change; it's reflective of a monumental shift in consumer preferences and shopping patterns.

Much of this unprecedented growth can be attributed to the unanticipated outbreak of the Coronavirus pandemic. The world as we knew it underwent a major shift and this transformation was especially felt in the area of commerce. With physical movement restricted and traditional retail avenues shuttered, online shopping emerged as a beacon of convenience and safety. What initially began as a necessity soon transformed into a lifestyle choice, fueling the expansion of the e-commerce landscape.

During this transformative period, platforms like Noon, Amazon, and a multitude of other e-commerce websites witnessed an astronomical surge in user activity. This wave of digital engagement showcased not only the adaptability of consumers but also the robust infrastructure that had been cultivated within the e-commerce ecosystem.

Delving deeper into the e-commerce landscape of the GCC, certain trends and categories have emerged as clear winners. Clothing, particularly ones with personalisation options, has experienced an overwhelming surge in demand. Consumers are now seeking products that resonate with their individuality and allow them to express their personal style in new and exciting ways.

Cosmetics and beauty products have also emerged as frontrunners in the e-commerce arena. The emphasis on natural and chemical-free formulations has resonated strongly with consumers who are increasingly health-conscious and environmentally aware. For businesses with products adhering to these values, the GCC market holds the promise of substantial success.

Addressing a regional concern, hair care products designed to combat hair fall have found a lucrative market. The distinctive water quality in the region has led to specific hair-related challenges for its residents. As a result, hair serums and related solutions have flourished, offering consumers a remedy to a persistent issue.

A fascinating facet of the GCC e-commerce landscape is the evident demand for niche and unconventional products. Items crafted from unique materials, such as the popularity of 100% bamboo products, have captivated the consumer base. This trend underscores the region's growing preference for products that are distinct, eco-friendly, and aligned with sustainable practices.

Chapter 2

UNDERSTANDING INTERNATIONAL MARKETS

2.1. RESEARCHING TARGET MARKETS

In our quest to understand how to excel in cross-border selling within the Gulf region, our first and foremost step is delving deep into the intricate world of market research. Without the right compass to navigate these uncharted waters, we may find ourselves lost in the vast ocean of opportunities and challenges.

The importance of market research should not be overlooked. It is the foundation upon which successful cross-border selling is built.

Imagine you are a seller on a renowned e-commerce platform like Amazon , Flipkart and other market places in India. While your domestic market is bustling with millions of sellers offering similar products, your gaze turns toward the Gulf region, where your product could potentially find a market three times its size.

But before you set sail, you must understand the terrain.

Research serves as your treasure map, guiding you toward hidden gems. In the Gulf Cooperation Council (GCC) countries like Saudi Arabia, the United Arab Emirates, Qatar, Oman, Bahrain, and Kuwait, demand for certain categories of products is soaring. By researching thoroughly, you can uncover these lucrative opportunities that may have remained hidden otherwise.

A crucial aspect of your research involves observing how the big giants have conquered the Gulf market. That is because they are like seasoned explorers who have navigated these waters successfully.

Take Amazon, for instance, which has an equivalent in the GCC called Noon. Analyse their strategies, the products they prioritise, and their customer engagement tactics. What can you learn from their journey? How can you apply their insights to your cross-border endeavours?

Certain product categories and websites hold immense sway in the GCC region. Your research should uncover the heavy hitters and the rising stars. By taking a closer look into the sales figures and market trends, you'll gain a comprehensive understanding of which categories are thriving. This insight is invaluable as it helps you align your product offerings with local preferences, ensuring you cater to the demands of the market.

In the game of cross-border selling, the geographical distance between your manufacturing unit and the target market is a critical factor. It's essential to assess how logistics will play a vital role in determining your selling price and cost price. Efficient logistics can be the wind beneath your sails, enabling you to offer competitive pricing and reliable delivery times, which are crucial for customer satisfaction.

After factoring in all the considerations mentioned above, suppose you've set your sights on the United Arab Emirates (UAE), a country with seven emirates. Your research should then shift focus to understanding the local population which is approximately 9.3 million.

Next, dig into the number of internet users among this population, for this is your potential customer base.

Discovering the average number of daily transactions in the UAE market will further refine your understanding of the market's dynamism and potential.

2.2. CULTURAL CONSIDERATIONS AND LOCALIZATION

In our exploration of cultural considerations and localization in cross-border selling in the Gulf region, we encounter an important aspect that cannot be overlooked: understanding and respecting the region's dietary and religious restrictions.

The Gulf region is characterised by its cultural diversity and strong adherence to religious beliefs. It's essential to acknowledge and respect these sensitivities when considering your product offerings. For instance, certain products, particularly those containing pork, may be restricted or even banned in some Gulf countries, such as the United Arab Emirates (UAE) due to Islamic dietary laws.

Pork is considered "haram" (forbidden) in Islam, and as such, its consumption and sale are prohibited in countries where Islamic law holds sway. UAE, being predominantly Muslim, adheres to these dietary restrictions, and the sale of pork-based products is strictly regulated. Therefore, if your business specialises in such products, it's crucial to research and understand the local laws and regulations.

If you find that your product lineup includes items that are restricted or banned in certain Gulf countries, it's wise to adapt your offerings accordingly. This demonstrates your commitment to respecting local norms and religious beliefs. Consider diversifying your product range to cater to local preferences, including halal-certified alternatives for food products.

Selling prohibited items can lead to severe legal consequences and damage your business reputation. Therefore, it's essential to consult with legal experts well-versed in the specific regulations of each Gulf country you intend to operate in. They can provide guidance on compliance and help ensure that your business operations remain within the bounds of the law.

While cross-border selling in the Gulf region presents exciting opportunities, it also demands a nuanced understanding of the cultural and religious sensitivities that shape the market.

By adapting to local norms, respecting religious beliefs, and complying with regulations, you can navigate a culturally sensitive market. After all, you want to ultimately ensure a positive and compliant presence in the Gulf market.

2.3.   LEGAL AND REGULATORY REQUIREMENTS

In our exploration of the intricate world of legal and regulatory requirements for cross-border selling in the Gulf region, we encounter a maze of rules and procedures that demand careful navigation. Understanding these requirements is essential for a smooth and compliant entry into this vibrant market.

Among the Gulf nations, the United Arab Emirates (UAE) stands out for its stringent legal environment. It's a jurisdiction where compliance is not an option but a necessity for doing business. The importance of adhering to legal norms cannot be overstated, and this chapter sheds light on some key aspects you must consider.

One of the fundamental requirements for doing business in the UAE is obtaining the appropriate licences. Without these licences, you may face hefty fines and potential business disruptions. The types of licences you require can vary depending on your business activities and the emirate in which you operate.

If your business operates in the realm of Business-to-Business (B2B) transactions, you must secure a trade licence. This licence is a prerequisite for conducting legal business in the UAE. It is essential regardless of whether you operate in a marketplace or sell specific products directly.

It's noteworthy that selling products that come into direct contact with the human body, such as cosmetics or medical devices, may require additional approvals. This ensures the safety and quality of products available in the market. Therefore, if your business falls into this category, be prepared for a thorough approval process.

To navigate the complex web of legal requirements efficiently, consider a strategic approach to product selection. Avoid starting with a broad range of products, especially if they differ significantly in size, colour, or other dimensions. Begin with a focused product line that complies with local regulations, and once established, gradually introduce variations.

Obtaining the necessary licences can be a difficult task, especially for newcomers. However, there are service providers and consultancies in the UAE that specialise in assisting businesses with the licensing process. They can streamline the procedure and ensure that you fulfil all requirements.

An interesting development in recent times is the Dubai Economic Department's initiative, which offers simplified licensing for certain businesses. It's reported that for a fee of 50,000 INR, businesses can obtain all the necessary licences to operate in Dubai. However, please note that the details and eligibility criteria for this initiative may change over time, so it's advisable to check with local authorities or a reputable consultant for the latest information.

In the Gulf region, securing a local bank account is often tied to having a trade licence. This means that to access local banking services, you must first meet the legal requirements for your business activities. This serves as an additional incentive to ensure compliance.

Maintaining compliance isn't a one-time affair. When your licences approach their renewal dates, you'll need to provide evidence of an operational office in the UAE. This underscores the commitment to local business presence and the importance of fulfilling legal obligations consistently.

In essence, while the legal and regulatory landscape in the UAE may seem formidable, it's navigable with proper guidance and understanding. The key takeaway is to approach the market with diligence, securing the necessary licences, and ensuring ongoing compliance. By doing so, you'll establish a strong legal foundation for your cross-border business. This will give you confidence about your success in the Gulf region.

2.4. PAYMENT METHODS AND CURRENCY EXCHANGE

In our exploration of cross-border selling in the Gulf region, we shall now delve into the critical aspects of payment methods and currency exchange. These elements are at the heart of ensuring trust, efficiency, and profitability in your business endeavours.

The Gulf region is home to various countries, each with its own currency. When conducting business in Qatar, for instance, transactions typically occur in Qatari Riyal (QAR). Understanding the currency preferences of your target market is essential to streamline your payment processes and cater to your customers effectively.

Before you embark on your cross-border selling journey, research and understand the intricacies of obtaining a trade licence in each Gulf country you intend to operate in. A simple online search can provide you with valuable insights and guidelines on the specific requirements and procedures for trade licensing in different regions.

Building trust with customers is a paramount consideration, especially when you are a new entrant in the market. Gulf consumers, like any others, may be hesitant to make upfront payments to unfamiliar businesses. To address this challenge, consider offering payment options that mitigate risk, such as Cash on Delivery (COD). COD is a widely accepted practice in the region, allowing customers to pay upon receipt of their orders, which can enhance their confidence in your business.

Cross-border payment logistics can be complex. While COD is a common choice for customer payments, it's essential to recognize that very few companies transfer funds to other countries, such as India, from Gulf countries. To facilitate these transactions, you'll typically need a local bank account in the Gulf region.

Currency exchange rates play a significant role in cross-border transactions. To ensure transparency and competitive pricing, consider displaying your product prices in local currencies, taking into account exchange rate fluctuations. However, be aware that some delivery companies may charge an additional 2% fee for currency conversion, so factor this into your pricing strategy.

Opening a local bank account in the Gulf region can streamline your financial operations and make cross-border transactions more efficient. This is particularly important if you plan to receive funds from customers or partners in the Gulf. Researching how to open a bank account in the UAE, for example, can provide valuable insights into this process.

Whether or not to open a local bank account should be influenced by your business's volume of transactions in the region. If you anticipate a significant volume of business in the Gulf, having a local account can offer cost savings and convenience.

The efficiency of your payment and delivery processes is closely linked to transit times and your choice of shipping companies. Quick and reliable shipping can positively impact customer satisfaction and payment processing. Therefore, selecting reputable shipping partners and optimising your logistics is a crucial aspect of cross-border selling success.

Mastering payment methods and currency exchange is pivotal to your cross-border selling venture in the Gulf region.

Every element of your business, from pricing to payment processing and delivery, contributes to building a solid reputation and ensuring a profitable and trustworthy presence in the Gulf market.

Chapter 3

SETTING UP AN E-COMMERCE BUSINESS IN UAE

3.1. BUSINESS REGISTRATION AND LICENSING

The United Arab Emirates, often referred to as the Emirates, is a Middle Eastern country consisting of seven emirates: Abu Dhabi, Dubai, Ajman, Fujairah, Ras Al Khaimah, Sharjah, and Umm Al Quwain. The majority of the U.A.E.'s population comprises expatriates, with nearly 7.8 million expats residing alongside 1.4 million Emirati citizens.

The U.A.E. offers a thriving and conducive business ecosystem characterised by political stability and favourable macroeconomic conditions. Notably, the World Bank Group's Doing Business 2023 Report ranks the U.A.E. as the 16th best country in the world for ease of doing business.

U.A.E. FREE TRADE ZONES (F.T.Z.S)

Free trade zones are designated geographic areas within each emirate where federal taxes, employment regulations, and import-export restrictions do not apply. In these U.A.E. Free Trade Zones (F.T.Z.s), bureaucratic requirements are streamlined, making them attractive investment destinations for foreign entrepreneurs.

There are over forty-five Free Zones spread across the U.A.E. Depending on your business requirements, office needs, and budget.

SO HOW DO YOU START A BUSINESS IN A FREE ZONE?

In the U.A.E. free zone, you can establish one of two types of businesses:

Free Zone Limited Liability Company (FZ LLC): This entity is a separate legal entity that can be formed by either individuals or corporate entities. The ownership and capital requirements will vary based on your company's size and domain of activity.

Free Zone Establishment (FZE): An FZE is a limited liability company, and its liabilities are limited to its capital. It has a distinct legal personality from its shareholder(s) and enjoys all the rights and privileges of an individual.

KEY DIFFERENCES BETWEEN FZE AND FZ LLC

FZE typically has a single shareholder, while FZ LLC requires two or more shareholders, with a maximum of five.

ADVANTAGES OF BUSINESS SETUP IN U.A.E. FREE ZONES

Setting up a business in one of the U.A.E.'s Free Trade Zones offers numerous advantages:

- Quicker company incorporation compared to setups outside the Free Zone
- Affordable labour force and streamlined recruitment procedures
- 100% foreign ownership
- 100% repatriation of capital and profits
- 100% free transfer of funds
- Full exemption from import and export duties
- Twenty-five-year lease options, availability of areas for production, warehousing, assembling, and more
- No currency restrictions
- Low freight charges

- Efficient single-window service and communication procedures

- Liberal government policies and a supportive legal system

- Abundant and affordable energy resources

- Notable U.A.E. Free Zones

LET US GET A DEEPER UNDERSTANDING OF SOME OF THE MOST PROGRESSIVE AND ADVANCED FREE ZONES IN THE U.A.E.

Abu Dhabi Free Zone: Known for its rapid growth and wealth, Abu Dhabi is an attractive market for business expansion. Free Zones within Abu Dhabi include Abu Dhabi Global Market Free Zone, Khalifa Industrial Zone (KIZAD), Masdar City Free Zone, and Abu Dhabi Airport Free Zone (ADAFZ).

Dubai Free Zone: Dubai's Free Zone Authorities handle registration formalities and issue business licences to non-resident or offshore companies. Free Zones in Dubai include Dubai Airport Free Zone, Dubai Design District, Dubai Humanitarian City, Dubai Metal and Commodities Centre, Dubai Investment Park (only through JAFZA), Dubai Silicon Oasis, Dubai Internet City, Dubai Media City, Dubai Healthcare City, Dubai World Central, Dubai Studio City, and more.

Ajman Free Zone: Ajman offers low-cost company registration opportunities and incentives for foreign investors. Free Zones in Ajman include Ajman Media City Free Zone and Ajman Free Zone.

Fujairah Free Zone: Situated in the eastern part of the U.A.E., Fujairah boasts strategic connectivity. Free Zones in Fujairah include Fujairah Creative City Freezone and Fujairah Free Zone.

Ras Al Khaimah Free Zone: Ras Al Khaimah Economic Zone (RAKEZ) provides local and foreign investors with access to various markets. It offers a strategic location and access to emerging markets.

Depending on your budget and the nature of your product you can choose the zone that feels most aligned with.

3.2. CHOOSING THE RIGHT E-COMMERCE PLATFORM

Lately, if you have taken a look at social media platforms like Facebook and Instagram have become popular choices for businesses to market and sell their products. While these platforms offer excellent visibility and audience engagement, relying solely on them may limit your sales potential. A dedicated landing page, accompanied by a well-structured sales funnel, can significantly enhance your online sales strategy.

THE PITFALLS OF SOCIAL MEDIA-ONLY SELLING

1. Limited Control: On social media platforms, you're bound by their rules and algorithms. Changes in these platforms' policies or algorithms can affect your reach and engagement, limiting your control over your online presence.

2. Competitive Environment: Social media is a crowded marketplace where businesses continuously compete for users' attention. It's easy for your products to get lost in a sea of posts and ads.

3. Dependence on Algorithm: Your product's visibility largely depends on the platform's algorithm, which can be unpredictable. Even if you have a sizable following, not all your followers will see your posts.

4. Lack of Data Ownership: When you rely solely on social media, you don't own the user data collected by

the platform. This can hinder your ability to target your audience effectively.

5. Limited Conversion Tools: While social media allows for product promotion, it lacks the advanced tools and customization options available on dedicated landing pages.

THE BENEFITS OF A DEDICATED LANDING PAGE

A landing page is a standalone web page designed for a specific marketing or advertising campaign. Here's why having one can really level up your business:

1. Full Control: With a landing page, you have complete control over its design, content, and functionality. You can tailor it to your brand and marketing goals.

2. Enhanced Conversion: Landing pages are designed to convert visitors into customers. You can implement specific call-to-action (CTA) buttons, forms, and other elements to drive conversions.

3. Data Collection: Collect valuable user data, such as email addresses, through landing page forms. This data can be used for personalised marketing and building customer relationships.

4. Improved SEO: Landing pages can be optimised for search engines, increasing your online visibility and attracting organic traffic.

5. Focused Message: A landing page allows you to deliver a clear and concise message to your audience, reducing distractions and improving the user experience.

BUILDING AN EFFECTIVE SALES FUNNEL WITH A LANDING PAGE

Now that we've established the importance of a landing page, let's delve into how to build an effective sales funnel around it:

1. Design an eye-catching and user-friendly landing page that aligns with your goal. Use compelling visuals, concise copy, and a persuasive CTA to capture visitors' attention.

2. Utilise various channels to drive traffic to your landing page. This can include social media promotion, email marketing, pay-per-click (PPC) advertising, or search engine optimization (SEO).

3. Include a lead capture form on your landing page to collect user information. Ensure it's easy to fill out and doesn't ask for too much information upfront.

4. Don't let them leave. Mesmerise them with offers they can't refuse. Provide something of value in exchange for user information. This can be a discount, ebook, webinar, or any other resource relevant to your audience.

5. Once you've collected leads, follow up with them through email marketing or other communication channels. Provide valuable content, build trust, and guide them through the sales process.

Make sure your landing page has the following features:

1. An introduction to your product or service as a solution to the visitor's problem or need. Highlight its benefits and how it can improve their life.

2. Include social proof, such as customer testimonials or reviews, to build trust with potential buyers.

3. Continuously track the performance of your sales funnel using analytics tools. Identify bottlenecks or drop-off points and make necessary optimizations to improve conversion rates.

Your job doesn't end after a sale. It just gets started.

HERE ARE 3 THINGS YOU NEED TO DO REGULARLY TO EFFECTIVELY USE YOUR FUNNEL

1. After a successful purchase, offer complementary products or upsells to maximise revenue per customer. Try retargeting through ads or send them an email with a discount code.

2. A/B testing can help you fine-tune your landing page and funnel. Experiment with different headlines, CTAs, and visuals to discover what resonates best with your audience.

3. Make it easy for customers to reach out for assistance if needed. Excellent customer service can lead to repeat business and referrals.

While social media platforms are valuable tools for marketing, relying solely on them to sell your products can limit your business's potential. A dedicated landing page, combined with a well-structured sales funnel, offers numerous benefits, including increased control, enhanced conversion rates, and improved data collection. Don't miss out on the opportunity to reach a broader audience and maximise your online sales potential with your own landing page. This brings us to our next topic of discussion — how to set up your store or landing page.

WHY SHOPIFY CAN BE YOUR BEST CHOICE FOR SETTING UP AN E-COMMERCE STORE

Among the numerous e-commerce platforms available, Shopify stands out as a top contender and, for many, the best choice.

1. User-Friendly Interface

   One of the primary reasons for Shopify's immense popularity is its user-friendly interface. You don't need to be a tech guru to set up your e-commerce store on Shopify. The platform offers an intuitive and straightforward dashboard that allows you to manage your products, customise your storefront, and track your sales with ease. Whether you're a seasoned entrepreneur or a novice, Shopify makes the setup process smooth and accessible.

2.   Beautiful and Customizable Templates

Your online store's appearance plays a crucial role in attracting and retaining customers. Shopify offers a wide range of professionally designed templates that cater to various industries and styles. These templates are not only visually appealing but also highly customizable. You can tailor them to match your brand's identity, ensuring your store stands out in a crowded marketplace.

3.   Mobile-Optimised

With an increasing number of consumers shopping on mobile devices, having a mobile-optimised website is essential. Shopify understands this trend and provides responsive templates that adapt seamlessly to different screen sizes. Your store will look and function just as well on smartphones and tablets as it does on desktop computers.

4.   Robust E-commerce Features

Shopify offers a comprehensive suite of e-commerce features designed to help you succeed. From product management and inventory tracking to order processing and customer management, Shopify covers all the essential aspects of running an online store. Additionally, the platform continually updates and improves its features, ensuring that you have access to the latest tools to enhance your business.

5. Payment Gateway Options

Providing a variety of payment options is crucial for accommodating your customers' preferences. Shopify integrates with numerous payment gateways, including PayPal, Stripe, and credit card processors, making it easy for you to accept payments securely and efficiently. The platform also supports multiple currencies, which is especially valuable if you plan to sell internationally.

6. Scalability

As your business grows, your e-commerce platform should grow with you. Shopify is highly scalable, allowing you to expand your product catalogue, handle increased traffic, and add new features as needed. You won't need to worry about outgrowing the platform or facing extensive migrations to more substantial solutions down the road.

7. SEO-Friendly

Search engine optimization (SEO) is vital for driving organic traffic to your online store. Shopify comes equipped with SEO features and tools that enable you to optimise your website for search engines. You can customise meta tags, titles, and URLs, and Shopify's clean code and responsive design contribute to better search engine rankings.

8. App Integration

Shopify's App Store offers a vast array of add-ons and integrations that allow you to extend your store's functionality. Whether you need email marketing tools, social media integrations, or analytics platforms, there's likely an app that suits your needs. This flexibility empowers you to tailor your store to your specific requirements.

9. Excellent Customer Support

Setting up and running an online store can be challenging, especially if you're new to e-commerce. Shopify provides excellent customer support with various avenues for assistance, including live chat, email, and a comprehensive knowledge base. You can count on timely and helpful responses to your queries, ensuring that you're never left stranded when facing challenges.

10. Security and Compliance

Protecting your customers' sensitive information is paramount in e-commerce. Shopify takes security seriously, offering SSL encryption, automatic updates, and compliance with Payment Card Industry Data Security Standard (PCI DSS) requirements. With Shopify, you can rest assured that your customers' data is safe and that you're meeting industry standards.

11. Cost-Effective

Starting a business involves managing expenses carefully. Shopify offers pricing plans that cater to various budgets. Whether you're just starting or running a large-scale operation, you can find a plan that suits your needs. Plus, the platform's transparency ensures that you won't encounter hidden fees or surprise charges.

12. Analytics and Reporting

To make informed decisions and optimise your store's performance, you need access to data. Shopify provides robust analytics and reporting tools that give you insights into your sales, customer behaviour, and website traffic. You can track your store's performance over time and make data-driven adjustments to improve your bottom line.

But of course, Shopify is not perfect. Otherwise, the other options would just stop existing.

DRAWBACKS OF USING SHOPIFY

While Shopify offers a robust platform for e-commerce businesses, it's important to be aware of its limitations to make an informed decision when selecting an e-commerce solution. Here are some of the key limitations of Shopify:

1. Monthly Subscription Costs: Shopify operates on a subscription-based pricing model. While it offers a range of plans to suit different budgets, the monthly fees can add up, especially for small businesses or startups. Additionally, the transaction fees for using external payment gateways can be an additional cost.

2. Transaction Fees: Unless you use Shopify Payments (which is not available in all countries), Shopify charges a transaction fee on each sale made through third-party payment gateways. These fees can cut into your profit margins, especially for high-volume businesses.

3. Limited Customization: While Shopify provides a range of customizable templates and themes, making deep design customizations might require coding skills or hiring a developer. Complete design freedom is somewhat limited compared to a fully custom-built website.

4. App Dependency: To extend functionality beyond what Shopify offers out of the box, you may need to rely on third-party apps from the Shopify App Store. While many apps are available, they can add costs and complexity to your store.

5. Platform Lock-In: If you decide to leave Shopify in the future, migrating your store to another platform can be challenging. Data migration and SEO preservation can be complex processes.

6. Limited Blogging Capabilities: While Shopify includes a blogging feature, it's not as robust as dedicated blogging platforms like WordPress. If content marketing and blogging are central to your strategy, this limitation might be a drawback.

7. Advanced SEO Control: While Shopify has improved its SEO features, it may not offer the same level of advanced SEO control and customization as some other platforms, which can impact your website's search engine ranking.

8. Multilingual Support: While Shopify supports multiple languages and currencies, achieving a truly multilingual and multi currency store can be complex and may require third-party apps or development work.

9. Limited Analytics in Lower Tiers: Advanced analytics and reporting features are only available in higher-tier plans, which means smaller businesses might not have access to detailed data.

Despite these limitations, Shopify remains an excellent choice for many e-commerce businesses due to its ease of use, scalability, and extensive ecosystem of apps and themes. Make sure you carefully evaluate your business's specific needs and goals to determine if Shopify is the right fit or if another e-commerce platform might better suit your requirements. But if you feel it is not for you there is another equally popular alternative.

Woocommerce gives you a level of freedom and customizability that Shopify can't provide. It is a plugin for WordPress that provides a more versatile and scalable solution.

Here are the top reasons why Woocommerce can be for you:

1. Cost-Effective: WooCommerce itself is free and open-source. While you'll still have expenses for hosting, domain registration, and potentially premium plugins, it's generally more cost-effective than Shopify.

2. Unlimited Customization: With WooCommerce, you have complete control over your website. You can customise every aspect of your store, from design to functionality, using WordPress themes and plugins.

3. Platform Independence: WooCommerce operates as a WordPress plugin, giving you more independence and control over your website. You can switch hosts and platforms with relative ease.

4. No Transaction Fees: WooCommerce doesn't charge any transaction fees, allowing you to keep more of your profits. You only pay payment gateway fees, which are standard in e-commerce.

5. Advanced SEO: WordPress, in combination with SEO plugins like Yoast SEO, offers advanced SEO capabilities. You can optimise your site's performance for search engines more effectively.

6. Blogging Functionality: If content marketing is essential to your strategy, WordPress (used alongside WooCommerce) offers superior blogging functionality, allowing you to create and manage engaging content seamlessly.

While Shopify is an excellent platform for many businesses, it's essential to recognize its limitations, especially as your e-commerce enterprise grows. WooCommerce, with its cost-effectiveness, customization capabilities, platform independence, and advanced SEO and blogging features, offers a robust alternative.

The good thing is that there are several popular shopping cart apps and platforms available in addition to Shopify and WooCommerce. These platforms cater to various needs and preferences, offering a range of features and customization options. Here are some of the notable ones:

1. Magento: Magento is an open-source e-commerce platform that is highly customizable and suitable for larger enterprises. It provides a wide range of features, including advanced SEO capabilities.

2. Wix eCommerce: Wix is known for its user-friendly website builder and offers a capable e-commerce platform. It's a good choice for smaller businesses looking for an all-in-one solution.

3. Squarespace: Squarespace is primarily a website builder, but it offers e-commerce functionality. It's an excellent choice for businesses that want an aesthetically pleasing website with ecommerce capabilities.

When choosing a shopping cart app or platform, consider factors such as your business size, budget, technical expertise, desired features, and scalability requirements. Each platform has its strengths and may be more suitable for specific types of businesses and e-commerce strategies.

3.3.   PAYMENT GATEWAY AND CURRENCY CONVERSION

Payment gateways are often overlooked while choosing ecommerce platforms even though that is one of the main centres of your business transactions. Your choice can significantly impact your profits, customer satisfaction, and overall business success. Let's see how we can choose the best payment gateway for your cross-border business.

Selecting the appropriate payment gateway for cross-border transactions is akin to choosing the right bridge to cross a river. A well-built bridge will get you to the other side safely and efficiently, while a poorly constructed one may lead to delays, losses, and even disaster.

Here's why your payment gateway choice matters:

1. Currency Handling: Cross-border transactions involve multiple currencies. A good payment gateway can seamlessly handle various currencies, ensuring customers can pay in their preferred currency, reducing conversion friction, and increasing sales.

2. Security and Trust: Trust is paramount in international transactions. A robust payment gateway provides top-notch security, protecting sensitive customer data and gaining their trust. An insecure gateway can lead to data breaches, eroding trust and reputation.

3. Transaction Costs: Payment gateways charge fees for their services. The right choice can help you minimise these costs, which can significantly affect your profit margins, especially in high-volume cross-border businesses.

4. Conversion Rates: A user-friendly and internationally recognized payment gateway can improve your conversion rates. Complex or unfamiliar payment methods may deter potential customers.

While choosing your payment gateway these are some of things you should be looking out for.

Choosing the best payment gateway for your cross-border business is more than a technical decision; it's a strategic one that can impact your bottom line and brand reputation. Prioritise factors such as currency support, security, user experience, and fees when making your choice.

3.4. LOGISTICS AND SHIPPING SOLUTIONS

This is the trickiest part, to be honest. This is where you do a lot of homework. No one understands your business better than you do. So you are the person who has all the relevant data required to make a decision on this front.

Expanding your business across borders can open up exciting opportunities for growth, but it also comes with its own set of challenges, particularly in the realm of logistics and associated costs. Understanding the intricacies of cross-border logistics is one of the first things you need to focus on for maximising profits and ensuring the sustainability of your international venture.

THE SIGNIFICANCE OF LOGISTICS IN CROSS-BORDER BUSINESS

1. Proximity Matters: One of the most significant factors impacting the cost and profitability of your cross-border business is proximity to your manufacturing source. Being closer to where your product is made can substantially reduce transportation costs. This proximity allows you to react faster to market demands, reduce lead times, and ultimately offer competitive prices.

2. Shipping Costs: Shipping costs can be a silent profit killer if not carefully managed. These costs include

transportation fees, customs duties, taxes, and handling charges. Ignoring or underestimating shipping expenses can erode your profit margins and even lead to losses.

3. Market Pricing: Understanding logistics can help you strategically price your products in different markets. For example, products may be cheaper in regions closer to manufacturing hubs due to reduced transportation costs. By adjusting your pricing strategy accordingly, you can attract more customers and increase market share.

STEPS TO MASTER CROSS-BORDER LOGISTICS

1. Conduct a Cost Analysis: Begin by thoroughly analysing all logistics-related costs, from manufacturing to delivery. Identify cost-saving opportunities, such as sourcing materials from nearby suppliers or establishing distribution centres in strategic locations.

2. Supplier Proximity: Evaluate the proximity of your suppliers to your manufacturing facility. If your supply chain is spread across different countries, consider consolidating it to reduce shipping and handling costs.

3. Choose the Right Shipping Method: Carefully select the shipping method that aligns with your business needs. Options like air freight, sea freight, or a combination of both can significantly impact costs and delivery times.

4. Negotiate Shipping Rates: Negotiate favourable shipping rates with carriers and freight forwarders. Bulk shipping and long-term contracts can often lead to better pricing terms.

5. Customs Compliance: Ensure your business complies with customs regulations and requirements in each target market. Mishandling customs documentation can lead to delays and additional costs.

Consider the example of Apple's iPhone pricing in different markets. iPhones are often more affordable in regions like Dubai, which is geographically closer to Apple's manufacturing hub in Asia. This proximity results in lower transportation costs, which are reflected in the retail price. Understanding this allows Apple to price its products competitively and attract a broader customer base.

Mastering logistics in cross-border business is not just about cost-cutting; it's about positioning your business for sustainable growth and profitability. Understanding the nuances of shipping methods can be a game-changer for your business, allowing you to offer products at a competitive price point—sometimes even 20% lower than prevailing market rates. I suggest to check quickshipme.com

When selecting a shipping partner, it's crucial to consider regional expertise. A certain company might be doing great in the UK. That does not mean they will be equally successful in the GCC. So if you are planning to expand your business in the GCC it would make zero sense to go with this company just because they have been successful in the UK market. It might be that they are selling the same product. However, a bigger factor to consider while making your decision is how well they understand your target market.

3.5. CUSTOMS AND IMPORT REGULATIONS

Each country boasts its own set of rules, regulations, tax structures, and benefits. To navigate these variables effectively, you need a shipping partner well-versed in the specifics of your target market. They should be capable of guiding you through the complexities and ensuring smooth operations. It's not just about shipping; it's about compliance and understanding the local business landscape.

Consider this scenario: you aspire to do business in the UAE, but you lack the necessary licence. Does this roadblock mean your dreams of expanding to the UAE must be abandoned? Absolutely not! There are innovative shipping partners that offer two-way shipping solutions. They seamlessly bridge the gap between your manufacturing source and the end customers within the UAE.

In this comprehensive e-commerce solution, you can essentially go hands-free. Your primary responsibilities revolve around marketing your products and driving sales. The rest—shipping, customs clearance, and delivery logistics—is expertly handled by your shipping partner. This approach not only circumvents licensing hurdles but also optimises your business efficiency.

By leveraging the expertise of regional players, adhering to local regulations, and exploring innovative solutions like two-way shipping, you can expand your business horizons without being encumbered by logistical constraints. Your focus remains on growth and customer engagement, leaving the complexities of international shipping in capable hands.

Chapter 4

PRODUCT SELECTION AND PRICING

4.1. IDENTIFYING PROFITABLE PRODUCT CATEGORIES

Understanding the international market can be a bit tricky as you are most likely unfamiliar with the sentiments and preferences of the people you are trying to cater to. But once you figure those out, it can provide tremendous value. By doing enough research you might come across products that are literally gold mines. I have had friends in the business who have selected a product on Amazon, created a separate landing page for that product, ran some ads and were selling it for 3X profit.

If you put some time into research, you too can find certain products that will require minimal effort from your end but make you a substantial profit. Your goal is to find a small range of products that have a high selling margin. Products sold by popular brands are generally not fit for this kind of venture. I suggest to check quicke.ae

4.2. FINDING AND PRICING THE 'RIGHT' PRODUCT

The world of e-commerce is an ever-evolving landscape, with product trends shifting like the seasons. Just as winter calls for cosy woollen attire, and summer beckons breathable cotton fabrics, the e-commerce realm is dictated by weekly trends akin to those you'd find in fast fashion retailers like Zara. In this expansive guide, we will delve into the art of identifying trending products with high-profit margins, offering you a blueprint for e-commerce success.

THE POWER OF TRENDING PRODUCTS

In the dynamic world of e-commerce, success is often synonymous with staying ahead of the curve. One of the most effective ways to achieve this is by tapping into trending products that capture the imagination of your target audience. These products not only pique consumer interest but also offer the potential for substantial profit margins.

IDENTIFYING TRENDING PRODUCTS: A STRATEGIC APPROACH

1. Market Research: The first step on your journey to uncovering trending products is thorough market research. Begin by scouting popular e-commerce platforms like Amazon, Noon.com, and even social media giants like Facebook.

    Actionable Tip: Search for the top-selling products within your chosen category on these platforms. Take note of the products that consistently rank high.

2. Leveraging Facebook Engagement: Facebook can serve as a valuable tool for product discovery. Explore the platform to identify which products are generating higher engagement rates among users.

    Actionable Tip: Pay attention to posts, comments, and shares related to specific products. These interactions are indicative of consumer interest.

3. Boosting Amazon Products: Amazon is a goldmine of product opportunities. You can enhance the appeal of existing Amazon products by creating better product videos that showcase their features and benefits.

    Actionable Tip: Invest in high-quality product videos that highlight key selling points, making your listings more appealing to potential buyers.

4. Evaluating Related Ads: To identify trending products, it's essential to keep an eye on advertisements related to your niche. These ads often spotlight products that are currently in demand.

Actionable Tip: Monitor ads on social media platforms and e-commerce websites. Take note of products being promoted and the strategies employed in these advertisements.

Exploring Online Marketplaces

5. AliExpress, Alibaba, and IndiaMART: Online marketplaces like AliExpress, Alibaba, and IndiaMART offer a treasure trove of product options. Explore these platforms to discover products that align with your niche.

Actionable Tip: Analyse product listings on these platforms to identify items with potential profit margins. Take note of product prices and shipping costs.

6. Google Trends: Google Trends is a powerful tool for gauging the popularity of specific products or search terms over time. This data can provide insights into the demand for particular products.

Actionable Tip: Enter keywords related to your niche into Google Trends. Review the search interest graph to assess whether interest is rising or declining.

Top Trending Product Websites

7. Top Trending Product Websites: Several websites are dedicated to curating lists of top trending products. These platforms can be invaluable for product discovery.

Actionable Tip: Make use of these websites to stay updated on the latest trends in the e-commerce world. Incorporate trending products into your offerings.

The Importance of Pre-Selling Research

8. Comprehensive Research Before Selling: Before adding a product to your inventory, it's crucial to conduct comprehensive research. This involves assessing product demand, profit potential, and market competition.

   Actionable Tip: Create a checklist that includes factors such as market demand, competitor analysis, and estimated profit margins. Only proceed with products that pass this evaluation.

Recognizing Platform-Specific Trends

9. Trends Vary Across Platforms: It's important to note that what's trending on one platform may not necessarily be trending on another. For instance, a product may be popular on TikTok but not gain the same traction on Instagram.

   Actionable Tip: Tailor your product selection and marketing strategies to the specific platform you are targeting. Consider the demographics and preferences of each platform's user base.

In-Depth Seller Analysis

10. Analyze Seller Rankings and Top-Selling Products: Investigate successful sellers in your niche to understand their strategies. Identify the top-selling products within their portfolios.

    Actionable Tip: Study seller profiles to uncover insights about their best-selling items, pricing strategies, and customer reviews. This knowledge can inform your product selection.

11. Cost Price Assessment: To accurately calculate profit margins, it's essential to know the cost price of the products you intend to sell.

Actionable Tip: Contact suppliers or manufacturers to obtain pricing details. Consider both product cost and shipping fees when calculating total expenses.

Harnessing Tools for Success

12. Adspy and Ads Library: Tools like Adspy and Ads Library can provide valuable insights into competitors' advertising strategies. They reveal which products are being promoted and for how long.

Actionable Tip: Utilise these tools to monitor ad campaigns in your niche. Gain insights into the duration and messaging of competitors' ads.

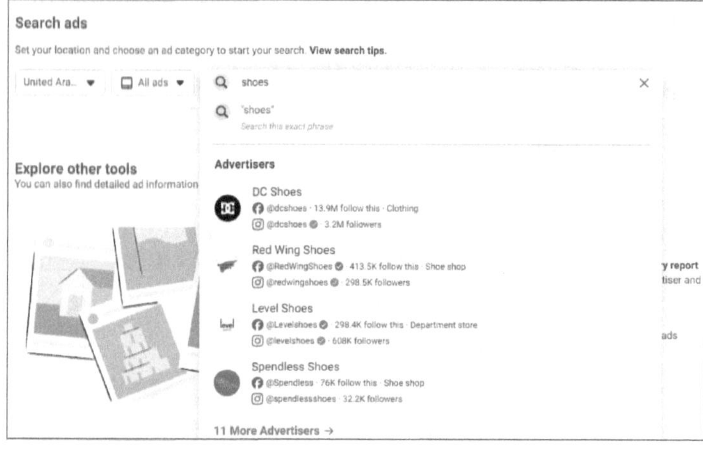

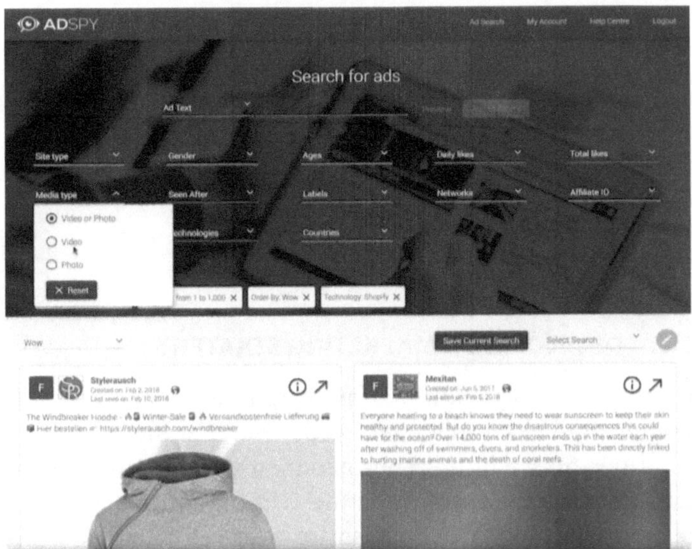

SORT BY 'WOW' REACTIONS WITH LIKES BETWEEN 1 AND 1,000. SEARCHES CAN BE AS COMPLEX AS YOU LIKE!

Through meticulous research, platform-specific analysis, and the use of powerful tools, you can uncover product opportunities that promise profitability.

While trends can be profitable, the key to long-term success lies in offering value to your customers. Building trust, providing exceptional customer service, and adapting to evolving consumer preferences will set you on a path to e-commerce prosperity.

Chapter 5

MARKETING AND PROMOTION

5.1. DEVELOPING A MARKETING STRATEGY

If you have a big dedicated marketing team then probably you are quite ahead in the game. But I want to provide solutions for even those businessmen who are just starting out, figuring their way into the GCC. I am talking about people who don't have an entire research team to figure things out. That is why I will give you a solid marketing plan that is going to be useful even if you are a seasoned player in this game.

This might sound repetitive but this is so important that I will say it again. You need to understand the products that you want to sell.

The local people of the GCC have a very specific outlook towards certain products. That naturally dictates the success of the particular product in the GCC market.

Let's take the example of clothes. People here prefer modest clothing irrespective of whether that is popular in the rest of the world. So even if you see a certain style of clothing in certain lucrative markets around the world that might not fly that well in the GCC.

The next thing you have to figure out is your budget. I cannot tell you what your budget should be but I will try my best to give you an idea of what steps you need to take depending on your budget.

If you have a high budget, then it makes a lot of sense to outsource marketing. You have to understand your primary business is tied to selling your product. That is your expertise. So it should come as a no-brainer that you would be saving a lot of time and effort if you can outsource your marketing endeavours to someone who is more familiar with the local sentiment. After all that is what makes marketing successful. Understanding people's sentiments and putting your message forward in a manner that influences those sentiments.

But not everyone has that kind of budget and the beautiful thing about this market is that you have just as high a chance of making it here with a lower budget. You just have to put in more effort and wear a couple of extra hats.

5.2. SEARCH ENGINE OPTIMIZATION (SEO) FOR THE GCC MARKET

Search Engine Optimization (SEO) is an indispensable tool for businesses looking to establish a strong online presence and drive sales in the Gulf Cooperation Council (GCC) region. The GCC is a rapidly growing market, and tapping into its potential requires a well-crafted SEO strategy tailored to the unique demands and preferences of this market. In this article, we'll explore the steps and considerations for developing a successful SEO plan to sell products in the GCC.

KEYWORD RESEARCH AND LOCALIZATION

Keyword Research: The first step in any SEO plan is keyword research. It's essential to identify the search terms and phrases that potential customers in the GCC region are using. These keywords should align with your product offerings. Tools like Google Keyword Planner and SEMrush can be immensely helpful in this phase.

Localization: Once you've compiled a list of relevant keywords, it's time to localise your content. The GCC has a diverse population, with Arabic being the most widely spoken language. However, variations in Arabic exist between countries. Tailor your content to reflect the specific dialects and language variations of your target audience.

OPTIMISING FOR MOBILE

In the GCC, mobile device usage is exceptionally high, making it crucial to optimise your website and content for mobile devices. Responsive web design ensures that your site is accessible and user-friendly across various screen sizes. Additionally, Google and other search engines prioritise mobile-friendly websites, making it a critical SEO factor.

QUALITY CONTENT CREATION

High-quality content is a cornerstone of successful SEO. In the GCC, it's essential to provide content that is not only informative but also culturally sensitive. Addressing the unique cultural norms and values of the region can enhance your brand's reputation and resonate with your target audience.

ON-PAGE SEO

Title Tags and Meta Descriptions: Create enticing title tags and meta descriptions for your pages, including relevant keywords. These are what users see in search results, so they should be compelling and relevant.

Header Tags: Use proper header tags (H1, H2, H3) to structure your content. This makes it more reader-friendly and helps search engines understand the hierarchy of your information.

Image Optimization: Optimise images by using descriptive file names and alt tags. This can improve your SEO rankings and enhance the user experience.

LINK BUILDING

Link building is a fundamental aspect of SEO. In the GCC, it's crucial to focus on building relationships with local websites and blogs. Seek out relevant, high-quality websites for guest posting opportunities, and create valuable content that naturally earns backlinks.

LOCAL SEO

For businesses operating in the GCC, local SEO is essential. Here's how to optimise for local searches:

Google My Business: Claim and optimise your Google My Business listing. This is a powerful tool for local SEO and will help your business appear in local searches.

Online Reviews: Encourage customers to leave reviews on platforms like Google and Yelp. Positive reviews can significantly boost your local SEO rankings.

Local Citations: Ensure that your business information (NAP - Name, Address, Phone Number) is consistent across all online directories and platforms.

E-COMMERCE AND PRODUCT PAGES

If you're selling products in the GCC, optimising your e-commerce and product pages is vital:

Product Descriptions: Craft unique and compelling product descriptions. Highlight the features and benefits of your products, and include relevant keywords.

User Reviews: Encourage customers to leave reviews and ratings for your products. Positive reviews can enhance your credibility and improve SEO.

Structured Data Markup: Implement structured data (schema markup) to provide search engines with additional information about your products. This can lead to rich snippets in search results, which can boost click-through rates.

REGULAR SEO AUDITS

To ensure the effectiveness of your SEO plan, conduct regular audits. Identify areas for improvement, update content, and adjust your strategy as needed. Search engine algorithms are continually evolving, and staying ahead requires adaptability.

ENGAGING IN SOCIAL MEDIA

In the GCC, social media plays a significant role in people's lives. Establish a strong presence on platforms like Facebook, Instagram, and LinkedIn. Sharing your content and engaging with your audience can boost your brand's visibility and, consequently, your SEO rankings.

Using Quickship you can do supercharge your content creation process leaving you with more time to work on strengthening the relationship between and your customers.

PAID ADVERTISING AND SEO

A comprehensive digital marketing strategy often combines SEO with paid advertising. Google Ads, for instance, can help you target specific keywords and demographics. When implemented strategically, paid advertising can complement your organic SEO efforts.

MEASURING AND ANALYSING RESULTS

To refine and improve your SEO strategy for selling products in the GCC, it's essential to measure and analyse results. Utilise tools like Google Analytics to track website traffic, user behaviour, and conversion rates. Regularly assess your rankings for targeted keywords and use the insights to make data-driven decisions.

5.3. SOCIAL MEDIA MARKETING AND INFLUENCER PARTNERSHIPS

Quite a significant bit of your marketing budget will be used in social media marketing and influencer partnerships.

If you are selling to real people and not businesses, you have to understand a simple psychology. People buy from people. So you have to involve real people in your marketing strategy who will communicate your product to your target customers. Social media influencers are best for this. They already have a user base that you can sell to. So all you are required to do is find the right influencer.

But who is the right influencer?

For that, you need to understand the influencers target audience. Who are the people following this person? What are their interests? What are they spending on?

If you are into the clothing industries the types of questions you should be asking is what kind of clothes does the influencer generally talk about that has led to them amassing such a huge following? If you are in the market to sell luxury products and the influencer's niche is cheap fast fashion, it is obvious that you two are not a good fit.

There is another catch to social media that you need to be aware of:

Not all social media are favoured by all. Certain apps are more popular with certain demographics, i.e. certain age groups, people of certain places, etc. So your target should be targeting those platforms that your target customers are more likely to frequent.

If your product has a strong visual aspect to it then you should be spending on platforms that cater towards a larger audience preferring visual content. TikTok and Snapchat are quite popular in the GCC. Instagram is not far behind either.

5.4.   ADVERTISING AND PROMOTIONAL CAMPAIGNS

If you have a limited marketing budget a lot of your work will involve emulating successful competitors. There is nothing wrong with not reinventing the wheel. It is actually an intelligent thing to do.

Your competitor has done all the research in your domain. They can show you what is working and what is not working. You just need to look in the right place and find the right competitors.

Thankfully platforms like Facebook Ads Library make this process so much easier. You will get a good idea of how you should be pricing your product and how you should be marketing your product.

In the digital age, businesses are increasingly shifting their marketing strategies towards mobile platforms to reach a wider audience. With a staggering 90% of purchases happening through mobile phones, it's evident that businesses must harness the power of mobile marketing to succeed. In this article, we will explore the dynamics of mobile marketing, with a particular focus on the GCC (Gulf

Cooperation Council) region. We'll delve into the role of social media campaigns, influencers, and advertising in bringing target customers to your site.

THE DOMINANCE OF MOBILE MARKETING

The prominence of mobile phones as a sales channel underscores the impact of mobile marketing. With mobile devices becoming ubiquitous, it's clear that a substantial chunk of customers are accessing products and services via their smartphones. To capture this vast market, companies are relying heavily on social media campaigns and YouTube channels to reach their potential buyers.

SOCIAL MEDIA: THE PREFERRED ROUTES

For most companies, social media campaigns and YouTube channels are pivotal in driving sales. These platforms offer a direct route to engage potential customers. In the GCC region, Facebook takes the lead, followed by Snapchat and TikTok. These platforms are the primary battlegrounds for marketers, and crafting strategies tailored to each platform's unique audience is crucial.

INFLUENCE OF INFLUENCERS

In addition to social media campaigns, influencers play a significant role in attracting the remaining 10% of purchases. Collaborating with local influencers is a popular tactic. These influencers bring authenticity and trust, making them instrumental in encouraging potential buyers to make a purchase. Businesses often incentivize influencers by offering them a percentage of sales, eliminating the upfront costs.

WHY ADVERTISING MATTERS

Advertising remains the cornerstone of mobile marketing. Companies that invest in advertising have a clear advantage over their competitors who may not be reaching their customers effectively. Mobile advertising on social media platforms not only helps you reach a broader audience but also allows you to target your ads specifically.

A/B TESTING AND COMPETITIVE ANALYSIS

Every platform provides tools for A/B testing, allowing you to experiment and refine your ad strategies. Competitive analysis is equally important. You can study competitors like 'quicke' to see which ads have been running successfully for an extended period. This data is invaluable, as it provides insights into what resonates with your target audience.

OFFERING PROMOTIONAL GOODIES

Seasonal festivities can be leveraged to provide promotional goodies to your customers. Businesses that are the first to market a product have a significant advantage, as they can tap into the excitement surrounding a new product's launch.

GOOGLE AND FACEBOOK BUSINESS MANAGER

These platforms offer precise tools to target your audience effectively. By using exact details, you can reach your potential customers with pinpoint accuracy. Additionally, keeping an eye on emerging trends and aligning your ad campaign with them is a surefire way to stay relevant.

Tools like Quickshipme's AI Image Generator and AI Copywriter helps you create attractive ads without breaking the bank. You can also do competitor analysis on the platform itself.

AI Image Generator
Marketing Module

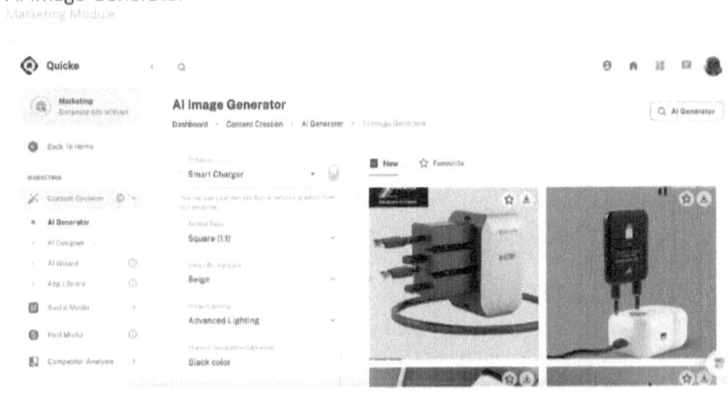

AI Copy Writer
Marketing Module

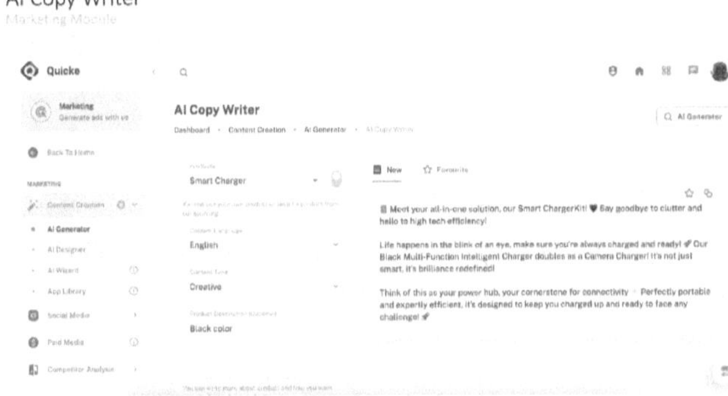

5.5. CUSTOMER ENGAGEMENT AND RETENTION STRATEGIES

NOT EVERYONE CLICKS ON EVERY AD

In the competitive world of digital marketing, not every click on an ad is guaranteed. Many factors contribute to this, including user preferences, ad relevance, and the user's intent at the time. However, understanding and harnessing the power of user engagement can significantly boost the effectiveness of your advertising efforts.

UNDERSTANDING USER INTENT

One crucial aspect to consider is user intent. People don't randomly click on ads; their interactions are often guided by their previous online activities. For instance, if someone has been actively searching for a specific product, such as a wallet, platforms like Facebook and Google already have data that indicates the user's interest in that product.

LEVERAGING HOT LEADS

These users represent what we call "hot leads." They are actively interested in a product or service, and their likelihood to convert into paying customers is higher. When someone clicks on an ad for a wallet, they leave a digital footprint, signalling their interest. This is where the real work begins for businesses looking to engage and retain these hot leads.

THE POWER OF RETARGETING

Retargeting, often offered as an option for ad managers, plays a vital role in customer engagement. It allows businesses to reconnect with potential customers who have previously interacted with their ads. In the case of the wallet ad clicker, retargeting ensures that your brand remains in the user's mind, increasing the chances of conversion.

IMMEDIATE RESPONSE WITH AUTO REPLIES AND CHATBOTS

In today's fast-paced world, immediate customer service is non-negotiable. With so many options at their fingertips, users have little patience for delays in response. This is where auto-replies and chatbots come into play. They allow businesses to initiate conversations with potential customers almost immediately.

By engaging with a prospective customer promptly, you increase the likelihood of keeping their attention and guiding them towards making a purchase. The key is to provide value and assistance quickly, ensuring that your company is the first to provide solutions to their needs.

RETAINING AND NURTURING CUSTOMERS

While attracting new customers is essential, retaining existing ones is equally, if not more, important. Newsletter subscriptions are a powerful tool for customer engagement. When someone has already made a purchase from your company, it's a clear sign of trust. Newsletters are a way to capitalise on that trust and continue building a long-term relationship.

SENDING TARGETED OFFERS

Newsletters provide an opportunity to send targeted offers and discount codes to your existing customers. These exclusive offers make customers feel appreciated and encourage them to continue shopping with your brand. The beauty of this strategy is that it can be executed without significant additional costs – you're essentially sending new offers to customers who have already demonstrated their interest in your products or services.

CUSTOMER RETENTION WITH REFERRAL PROGRAMS

A customer referral program is a fantastic way to engage and retain customers while also attracting new ones. By rewarding existing customers for referring friends and family, you create a sense of community around your brand. For example, offering a cashback incentive, such as "Give them 5 friends' references, and get 30 dirhams cashback on your next purchase," encourages your customers to actively promote your products or services.

These programs not only enhance customer engagement but also contribute to customer loyalty. When your customers become advocates for your brand, they are more likely to remain with you for the long haul.

Chapter 6

STEP-BY-STEP GUIDE TO DIGITAL MARKETING

Enough theory. Let's get your feet wet. In this chapter we will set up our Facebook page and connect it to our website (In chapter 3 we discussed where and how to get a landing page for your business).

The best part is you can do most of what we do now just from your phone.

STEP 1: CREATING A FACEBOOK PAGE FOR YOUR BUSINESS

1. Log into Your Personal Facebook Account:

    Begin by logging into your personal Facebook account. If you don't have one, you'll need to create one to manage your business page.

2. Navigate to Facebook Pages:

    Once logged in, go to the "Create" section on the top right-hand corner of your Facebook homepage. Select "Page" from the dropdown menu.

3. Choose Page Type:

    Select the appropriate page type for your business. Options include "Business or Brand," "Community or Public Figure," or others. Fill in the necessary details, including your business name and category.

4. Complete Business Details:

    Provide additional information about your business, such as a brief description, contact details, and a profile picture. Make sure your profile picture and cover photo are reflective of your brand.

5. Create a Username:

    Choose a unique username for your page. This will help users find and tag your business more easily. Ensure it's simple, memorable, and relevant to your brand.

6. Add a Call-to-Action Button:

    Facebook allows you to add a call-to-action (CTA) button to your page. Options include "Shop Now," "Contact Us," and more. Choose a CTA that aligns with your business goals.

7. Customize Your Page:

    Explore the customization options provided by Facebook. Add relevant tabs, such as "Shop," "Reviews," and "About." This helps users navigate your page and learn more about your business.

8. Publish Your Page:

    Once satisfied with the setup, click on the "Publish" button to make your page live. Congratulations, you've successfully created your business page on Facebook!

STEP 2: CONNECTING YOUR FACEBOOK PAGE TO YOUR BUSINESS LANDING PAGE

1. Access Page Settings:

    Navigate to your Facebook page and click on "Settings" in the top right corner.

2.   Edit Page:

Under "Settings," click on "Edit Page" in the left-hand menu. Choose "Settings" and scroll down to find the "Country Restrictions" section.

3.   Remove Country Restrictions:

If you intend to reach a global audience, ensure there are no country restrictions. Remove any limitations to maximize your page's visibility.

4.   Add Website Link:

In the "About" section, add the link to your business landing page. This creates a direct connection between your Facebook page and your website.

5.   Verify Your Website:

To enhance credibility, verify your website on your Facebook page. This involves adding a piece of code to your website or linking your domain to your Facebook account.

6.   Set Up Shop Section:

Since your business involves selling products, you should set up the "Shop" section on your Facebook page. This allows users to browse and purchase items directly from your page.

STEP 3: ADDING POSTS TO YOUR WEBSITE AND BOOSTING INTERACTION

1.   Create Engaging Content:

Craft content that resonates with your target audience. This could include product updates, behind-the-scenes glimpses, and relevant industry news.

2. Embed Facebook Posts:

   Share your Facebook posts directly on your website by embedding them. This not only adds dynamic content but also encourages visitors to engage with your Facebook page.

3. Encourage Comments and Shares:

   Prompt audience interaction by posing questions in your posts. Encourage users to share their thoughts and experiences. Respond promptly to comments to foster a sense of community.

4. Run Contests and Giveaways:

   Boost engagement by organizing contests or giveaways exclusively for your Facebook audience. Redirect users to your website to participate, increasing traffic and interaction.

5. Utilize Facebook Insights:

   Regularly check Facebook Insights to understand your audience's preferences. Tailor your content strategy based on the type of posts garnering the most engagement.

6. Cross-Promote Content:

   Share snippets of your website content on Facebook and vice versa. This cross-promotion strategy enhances visibility across platforms and drives traffic.

7. Implement Social Sharing Buttons:

   Add social sharing buttons to your website posts, making it easy for visitors to share content on their Facebook profiles. This amplifies your reach within their social circles.

8. Run Facebook Ads:

    Consider running targeted Facebook ads to drive traffic to your website. Use compelling visuals and persuasive copy to entice users to click through.

    By diligently implementing these steps, you'll not only establish a robust presence for your business on Facebook but also seamlessly integrate it with your business landing page. This interconnected approach enhances brand visibility, increases customer engagement, and helps your cross-border selling venture move towards sustained success.

Chapter 7

FULFILMENT AND LOGISTICS

Effective customer service is not confined to interactions with buyers alone; it extends to the management of critical operational aspects that impact customer satisfaction. This chapter delves into four pivotal elements within the customer service and support framework.

7.1. INVENTORY MANAGEMENT

Inventory management is the heartbeat of any successful cross-border selling venture. Imagine purchasing 10 units but selling only 3 or, conversely, experiencing unexpected demand exceeding your inventory. This is where a robust inventory management system becomes indispensable.

The importance of real-time tracking cannot be overstated. As a seller, having a comprehensive understanding of available stock in specific regions allows you to make informed decisions. For instance, if you have 100 pieces allocated to Saudi Arabia, you can initiate order dispatch once you're confident in the inventory status.

Inventory management involves more than just tracking quantities; it involves agility and adaptability. When shipments are incomplete or orders need modification, a sophisticated system allows you to make seamless adjustments, such as changing addresses or substituting products within existing orders.

Understanding the intricacies of inventory management is crucial in navigating hidden charges associated with warehousing. Some companies bill separately for stocking, airway bills, and processing. It's advisable to negotiate a lumpsum amount that encompasses all relevant charges, including storage, dispatch, and packing.

7.2. WAREHOUSING AND FULFILLMENT OPTIONS

Fulfillment is the bridge between an order and its successful delivery. It involves a series of crucial steps: order receipt, product labeling, packaging, and handover to a courier company. All these operations are typically managed within a warehouse.

The significance of choosing the right warehousing and fulfillment partner cannot be overstated. Opting for a reputable provider ensures efficiency in operations, but multinational companies may lack flexibility and personalized service. Dedicated account managers are often replaced by automated systems, limiting the adaptability needed for cross-border selling.

Local providers or courier aggregators, on the other hand, offer more flexibility and a range of options. Engaging with multiple courier companies, perhaps 20-30, provides a safety net. If dissatisfaction arises with one, alternatives are readily available. Some providers may offer additional benefits like free warehousing for utilizing their services for the last-mile delivery.

7.3. SHIPPING CARRIERS AND LOGISTICS PARTNERS

Selecting the right shipping carriers and logistics partners is a strategic decision that directly impacts customer satisfaction. While multinational carriers may offer reliability, their lack of flexibility can be a drawback. The absence of dedicated account managers and a tendency to return undelivered packages to the origin can create challenges for businesses of smaller scale.

For cross-border selling, especially in the early stages, engaging with local or courier aggregator services presents a more dynamic solution. These providers offer a wider range of options, allowing sellers to adapt to the diverse demands of international shipping. The ability to negotiate domestic charges and navigate the intricacies of local customs contributes to a smoother and more cost-effective shipping process.

7.4. DEALING WITH CROSS-BORDER RETURNS

Returns are an inevitable aspect of cross-border selling, and managing them efficiently is a crucial component of customer service. When dealing with returned shipments, it's essential to integrate them seamlessly into local inventory to avoid unnecessary complications.

For sellers opting for cash-on-delivery (COD) due to customer reluctance to provide credit card information, delivery performance becomes a critical factor. Reputed companies might not notify you of undelivered items and simply return them to the origin. To prevent this, establishing a local inventory and fulfilling new orders from this stock ensures continuous service and access to domestic charges.

In instances where shipping companies do not provide the required facilities, collaborating with local partners becomes an effective workaround. By partnering with a third party, businesses can request the shipping company to deliver the products to the local partner's facility, enabling seamless inventory management and order fulfillment.

The synergy between customer service and operational efficiency is paramount in cross-border selling. From managing inventory intricacies to selecting the right logistics partners, a comprehensive approach to customer service ensures not only customer satisfaction but also the smooth functioning of the entire cross-border selling ecosystem.

Inventory
Sourcing Module

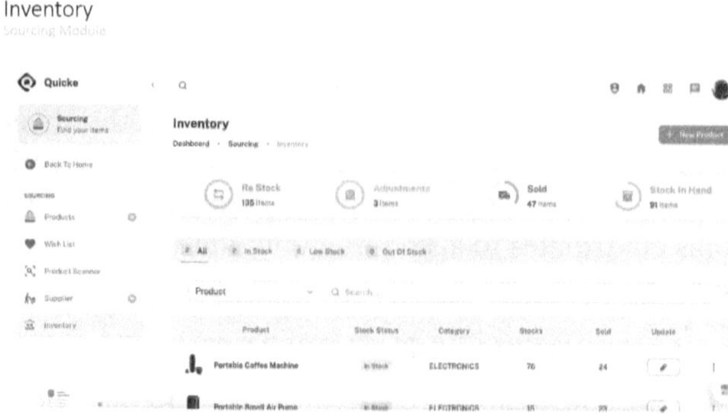

Quickshipme makes the entire process seamless

Chapter 8

CUSTOMER SERVICE AND SUPPORT

If you want to set your business apart from the rest in cross-border selling, effective customer service and support are critical components that you just can't underplay. This chapter delves into three essential aspects of customer service in the context of marketing through Facebook and TikTok, specifically focusing on handling customer inquiries and complaints, managing returns and refunds across borders.

8.1. HANDLING CUSTOMER INQUIRIES AND COMPLAINTS

In the age of social media marketing on platforms like Facebook and TikTok, customer interaction is the cornerstone of building a successful business. These platforms offer diverse avenues to engage potential customers, redirecting them to your website, landing pages, or communication channels like WhatsApp and Messenger.

Customers today seek more than just a transaction; they crave interaction and personalised experiences. As a cross-border seller, it's crucial to recognize the power of effective customer service in converting inquiries into confirmed orders. Given that you may be dealing with relatively inexpensive products, your customer service team becomes an invaluable resource for providing information not readily available online.

With potential customers attracted by promotional videos, the need for responsive and well-trained customer service becomes apparent. Unfortunately, the guidelines on these platforms may restrict the content of promotional videos, making it challenging to convey all necessary details. Customer service steps in to bridge this gap, offering additional information, customer reviews, and addressing queries that the promotional content couldn't cover.

8.2. MANAGING RETURNS AND REFUNDS ACROSS BORDERS

Cross-border selling introduces complexities in managing returns and refunds. Your customer service team plays a pivotal role in navigating these challenges. Inexpensive products may not always have comprehensive online information. Hence there is a need for a knowledgeable customer service team to guide customers through the returns process.

Effective communication regarding return policies, international shipping, and refund procedures is something to work towards. Transparency in these processes helps build trust with customers, creating long-term relationships. The ability of your customer service team to handle returns seamlessly contributes to a positive customer experience, reinforcing your brand's credibility.

8.3. PROVIDING PRODUCT INFORMATION AND RECOMMENDATIONS

As we discussed earlier, in social media marketing, especially when dealing with products that may have restrictions on promotional content, customer service becomes a strategic tool for providing information. Potential customers, drawn in by captivating videos, often have questions about the product's features and suitability for their needs.

Your customer service team should be well-versed in the products you offer, equipped to address inquiries, and provide valuable recommendations. They act as the human touchpoint that goes beyond the limitations imposed by platform guidelines. For instance, if marketing regulations prohibit specific claims, your customer service team can share detailed information, customer testimonials, and before-and-after experiences upon direct interaction.

8.4. THE INTERCONNECTED ROLES OF MARKETING AND CUSTOMER SERVICE

While some may argue that the activities described are more aligned with marketing, the reality is that, especially in the early stages or for solo entrepreneurs, there may be a blending of roles. Your team might need to wear multiple hats, including marketing and customer service. The emphasis is on recognizing the symbiotic relationship between these functions in the context of cross-border selling.

Your customer service team becomes the linchpin in converting potential customers into repeat buyers. The personalized touch, facilitated through one-on-one interactions on platforms like TikTok, distinguishes your business from larger competitors. Building relationships and trust is a luxury that smaller enterprises can afford, setting them apart in a market saturated with impersonal transactions.

In an era where social media platforms serve as the battleground for customer attention, mastering the art of customer service is non-negotiable. Your team's ability to handle inquiries, navigate international returns, and provide insightful product information directly impacts your brand's success. As a cross-border seller, you have the unique opportunity to leverage customer service not just as a reactive function but as a proactive force. This will help you propel your business towards sustained growth and customer loyalty.

CONCLUSION

When we talk about cross-border selling, we need to think beyond the present market. We should be capable of seeing what lies ahead. This chapter explores potential growth opportunities and leaves you with some rock-solid recommendations to ensure the success of your cross-border e-commerce venture.

FUTURE GROWTH OPPORTUNITIES

Establishing your business in different countries isn't just a good idea; it's a strategy that can propel your business to new heights. Think about the giants—those companies that seem to touch every corner of the globe. They didn't get there by chance; they got there by leveraging scalability and replicability.

Mastering cross-border commerce in one nation unlocks the potential to replicate that success elsewhere. As an example, imagine navigating the bustling commercial landscape of the Emirates, then transitioning to the established marketplaces of Saudi Arabia. This experience equips you with a deep understanding of the intricacies involved in cross-border trade.

Now, replicate that. Conduct the same meticulous research for every country you set your eyes on. The origin remains constant; it's the destination that changes. You just need to find reliable partners who can deliver the goods.

Focus your scaling efforts on the countries that show promise, the ones where your products are flying off the virtual shelves. It's like planting seeds in different soils—some will yield a more abundant harvest.

As your sales climb, consider seeking funding. Once you start making somewhere between 25,000 INR to 30,000 INR daily, start exploring opportunities for investment. Use these funds wisely, not just to fulfill orders but to invest in your brand. Branding is your business's face, and a recognizable face goes a long way in the world of e-commerce.

Expand your product sourcing. Diversify your offerings. The more variety you bring to the table, the wider your customer base becomes. It's not about making huge shipments to one country; it's about making smaller, strategic shipments to multiple countries.

Look into platforms that offer integration without the need for hefty upfront payments. These platforms can be your allies in expanding your reach without stretching your budget thin. Always be ready to adapt. The more you can adapt to different market variations the faster you will be able to grow.

FINAL RECOMMENDATIONS

Now, let's distil all the insights and experiences into some straightforward recommendations:

1. **Local Shipping Partners are Key:** It might sound like a broken record, but it's crucial—find local shipping partners. Even at the destination, having a local partner can streamline the process, ensuring smoother deliveries and fewer headaches.

2. **Niche Down Your Products:** Spend a considerable amount of time figuring out what products can truly resonate in a particular country. You don't

want to sell everything to everyone. Instead you need to offer and deliver precisely what your target audience craves.

3. **Invest in Customer Sales Support:** This is your secret weapon. Your customer service team is not just there to field complaints; they are responsible for helping your build relationships. Make sure they are in constant touch with you throughout the process.

4. **Communication is Gold:** Stay in touch with your customers. Let them know where their package is in the entire journey. Your aim is not just to deliver a product, you need to deliver an experience. This is how you turn a one-time buyer into a recurring customer.

5. **Build Relationships:** Numbers are just a part of cross-border e-commerce success. But a bigger part is made by the people. If you have 200 loyal customers and 50 of them buy regularly, you're not just a seller; you're a successful entrepreneur. When you build relationships people become your ambassadors. They start seeing your success as their success.

The road to cross-border e-commerce success is paved with scalability, adaptability, and strong relationships. Be open to new opportunities, and don't forget the people behind the orders—your customers. Here's to your success in expanding your business through cross-border selling!

...